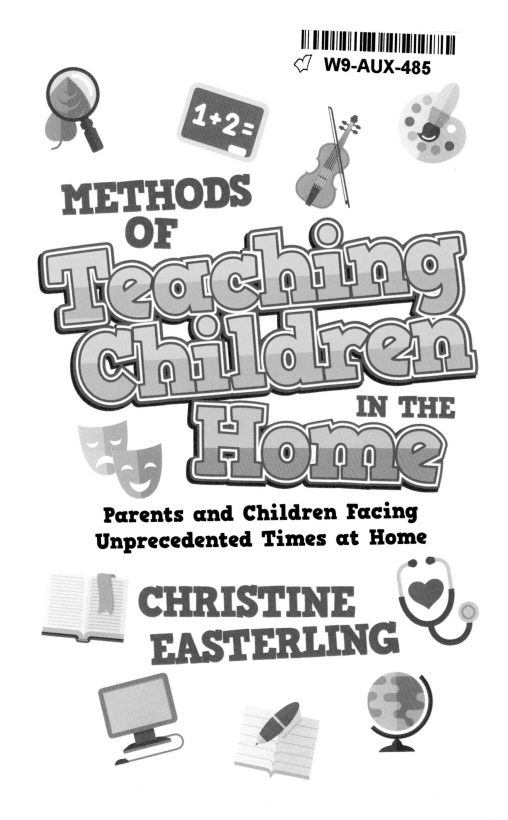

METHODS OF Teaching Children IN THE Home

Parents and Children Facing Unprecedented Times at Home

CHRISTINE EASTERLING

By the Same Author

Inspirational Treasures: Essays by Educators and the Students

Reflecting the Joys of Teaching

A Giant for Justice: Inspirational Biography of William H. "Bill" Simons III

Divine* Miraculous* Magnificent: The Miracles of Jesus

You Can Move Your Mountains:
Keep Pushing Your Mountain-Moving Faith

CONTENTS

DEDICATION

I write this dedication to those who made it all possible for me to step up and help parents and children during unprecedented school closings by writing this book.

I dedicate this book to my mother, Harriet Ann Davis, and my father, Lynwood Davis Jr. who left fingerprints of grace on my life. They will not be forgotten.

I further dedicate this book to my family and the teachers, parents, children, the government, the media, organizations, and corporations of America who, like me, thought it was their duty to step up and assist after unprecedented school closings.

I am especially indebted to teachers, Sandra Gilchrist, Teresa Austin and vice principal Cynthia Webb who poured out their hearts to me extensively about their role during the Pandemic crisis and school closings in addition to publisher Thelma Austin who continued to encourage me to write this book. I further dedicate this book to my little niece, Di'trinae Pettis whose picture is on the show and tell page, to my niece Tramiyah Clark in the reading and physical fitness section of this book and Austin Walker in the grocery store math section of chapter 19. I applaud them for their success in school as honor roll students every year. They are all elementary school students and victims of school closings.

PREFACE

Because I taught school for 16 years and served as a vice principal and director of a teaching academy for 14 years, I felt sympathy for the students who would suffer detachment from their teachers, would react to sudden disruption in their education, would suffer feelings of helplessness, loss of control, uncertainty and disruption because of unprecedented changes resulting from the Corona Virus Pandemic.

The pandemic was so devasting to the whole world, that I felt compelled to help in the best way I could relative to my own talents and skills. I wanted to focus on the solutions rather than the problem, and therefore started writing a book that would address methods of teaching children outside of the home. I thought that a book of this nature might help students and parents during an unprecedented crisis. I thought it to be my duty as a retired educator to continue to address educational issues. How could I do more?

Because of the pandemic resulting in the sudden closing of school, children felt disconnected from their teachers, and teachers and parents had to take on new roles. Because of the uncertainty, social distancing, isolation, confinement, sudden learning interference, psychological reactions, and family life disruption children are facing, I thought that children needed adequate teaching and learning routines that my book would help facilitate.

Moreover, children and parents need support after being suddenly thrust with distance learning, YouTube, Zoom, iPhone, Chrome Books, See Saw, Google classroom, etc., in addition to uncertainty about getting meals. Schools are happy places for children, and social distancing frustrates children who need all the love and attention they can get from school and home.

In order to aid children who experience sudden school closure, some teachers used distance learning, and Google classrooms, but wrestled with their feelings about saying goodbye to children while children experienced sadness about leaving their teachers as they try to focus on YouTube, WIFI, Learning Packets, home workbooks, county websites, in addition to a whole new learning required in logging onto educational computer systems.

The Seattle School Superintendent, in her response to the district's coronavirus, said: "Education is a service to which our district is resolutely committed. It is not a place," Reid wrote in her statement announcing the closure. "To that end, we are shifting our education from the classroom with four walls to the cloud. We are taking this strategic approach not because we think by doing so, we will stop an epidemic; we are simply trying to do our part to slow the spread of COVID-19."

Whether online or on paper, teachers, parents, and the world need to help meet children's social, academic, emotional, and physical needs during unprecedented times.

Because school closure put a halt to the structure of the systematic academic learning of children, as a retired educator I was compelled to help address some of the many issues relative to the pandemic. I chose to write a book to address education in the home.

Included in this book are: chapters such as homeschooling schedules, computer safety, home art, music drama, art, dramatics, kitchen math, physical fitness, health, speaking, reading, writing, spelling, social studies, outdoor science, and rewarding children. It also addresses how educators, organizations, companies, institutions, and states step up after sudden, unprecedented changes resulting from a pandemic—an infectious disease that spreads through human populations across large regions, such as an entire continent.

I wish to help families that are left struggling to find ways to teach and entertain their children while also going about the routines of daily living during challenging times of a pandemic. This book offers families more guidance on how to better engage their children in meaningful learning as they go through daily living activities, in addition to showing them how children can learn from experiences outside of the classroom.

ACKNOWLEDGMENTS

I give credit to scholars such as Larsen, Walsh, Almond, and Myers, who found that teaching and learning experiences that take place outside of the confines of the classroom walls have a range of benefits for both students and instructors. When children are asked to put into practice "in the real world" what they have theorized about from behind a desk, the result is a student-centric learning experience that enhances learning and fosters personal and social development (Larsen, Walsh, Almond, & Myers, 2017). They profess that, children who engage in learning experiences outside of the classroom have higher levels of motivation, recall the course material more vividly, and have improved academic performance in the class (Takeuchi et al., 2016; Ryan and Deci, 2017).

I further acknowledge television and radio stations, such as CBS, MSNBC, Fox, and organizations such as the Washington Teachers Union for distance learning, the American Federations of Teachers, and others who took the lead in addressing the issues of the pandemic resulting in school closings.

Families should think of homeschooling activities as field experiences, which can be formative and can inspire students to continue their education, rather than as activities that are a burden to bear (Hutson, Cooper, & Talbert, 2011).

Learning experiences outside the classroom are forms of experiential learning (Dewey, 1897). These experiences are rooted in the simple principle that "experience is the best teacher." Under this framework, learning outside of the classroom is an active process, wherein students encounter authentic problems, construct novel hypotheses, test for real solutions, and interact with others to make sense of the world around them. When we do this, we encounter the world as a whole and are forced to engage multiple modalities, no matter which pair of disciplinary "lenses" we intend to wear. Because experiential learning is inherently interdisciplinary, scientists and humanists alike would do well to consider the ways in which other disciplines might enrich their own disciplinary approach to their field.

I would like to express my gratitude to those support systems that have been the source of numerous thoughts and illustrations in this book. I especially acknowledge the families of the children who appear in this book: Tammy Clark Brown, Teresa Austin, Katrina Knight, Thomas Knight, Tramar Clark, and Monique Jackson.

INTRODUCTION

Corona means "crown" in Spanish, and coronavirus is a category of viruses so named because of its appearance—it's covered with crown-like spikes, according to the Atlanta-based Centers for Disease Control and Prevention. The outbreak was thought to have started at a food market in Wuhan, China, located close to the laboratory (credit: AFP or licensors). The first scientific evidence revealed that the virus did come from bats and is a version of SARS, a pandemic in 2002–2003 that killed 774 people.

Two new scientific studies, published in the journal *Nature*, have together provided the first formal evidence on the deadly new illness. Their findings confirm that the Wuhan coronavirus is a type of SARS, but one that can spread more easily.

School closures put an incredible strain on working parents, strapping them with the responsibility to explain the pandemic to their children and also making arrangements for last-minute child care to teach their children at home on short notice.

Parents had to learn information so they could explain it to their children. Thankfully, The National Association of School Psychologists and the National Association of School Nurses put out detailed guidelines for parents in late February explaining that when it comes to talking to kids about a pandemic, it's best to reassure them while also providing "factual, age-appropriate information about the potential seriousness of disease risk and concrete instruction about how to avoid infections and spread of disease."

For younger children, the guide says, it's best to give "brief, simple information that should balance COVID-19 facts with appropriate reassurances." Give simple examples of the steps people take every day to stop germs and stay healthy, such as washing hands. Use language such as "adults are working hard to keep you safe," the guide says.

Older children, meanwhile, are "able to discuss the issue in a more in-depth (adult-like) fashion and can be referred directly to appropriate sources of COVID-19 facts. Provide honest, accurate and factual information about the current status of COVID-19. Having such knowledge can help them feel a sense of control," the guide says.

Los Angeles Unified announced that it will open 40 family resource centers to provide care for children if families need it. These centers would provide child care, educational activities, and other services and packaged meals.

The Centers for Disease Control and Prevention has also offered a list of guidelines for talking to kids about coronavirus. They include:

1. Remain calm and reassuring.
2. Make yourself available to listen and to talk.
3. Remember that viruses can make anyone sick, regardless of a person's race or ethnicity.
4. Pay attention to what children see or hear on television, radio, or online.
5. Consider reducing the amount of screen time focused on COVID-19 and provide information that is honest and accurate.
6. Give children information that is truthful and appropriate for the age and developmental level of the child.
7. Talk to children about how some stories on COVID-19 on the internet and social media may be based on rumors and inaccurate information.
8. Teach children everyday actions to reduce the spread of germs.

However, all of this does not totally remedy the emotional problems and the suddenness of closing schools suffered by both the parents and the children. Closing schools amid a virus outbreak was scary for the parents and the children.

Therapist Jonathan Vickburg, the mental health supervisor with Cedars-Sinai's Share and Care program, said that as parents and caregivers navigate the new reality, it will help children if adults would look for ways to lessen their own fears. He went on to say that when we as adults have our anxiety on high alert, it is so easy to project that onto kids. What happens sometimes is the kids are trying to reduce that anxiety and they're trying to take care of us, and it should not be that way. "Right now, it really is, as adults, how do we ground ourselves and resource ourselves and feel confident that we can be there for our kids?" Vicksburg said it can be helpful to think of the things that have reduced stress in the past — maybe it's reaching out to friends, religion, therapy, or turning off the news every once in a while. Sharing those solutions with kids can also be helpful, he said.

"You can tell them, 'I was nervous too, and this is what I did,'" Vicksburg said. "It's a way to model for our kids."

And, Vicksburg said, if kids do have questions, adults should answer them with facts that are developmentally appropriate.

"Don't try to hide information," he said. "Some parents feel, 'If I give them all of that, it's going to scare them.' But the message that's conveyed if parents don't give information is that it's too scary for even parents to talk about."

If children are going to be home a lot more, it also helps to find ways to keep them active and make for family time.

"It can be something like, 'We're going to be home, and maybe you kids can help me make some of the dinner,'" he said. "It's a way of making the situation not as scary."

And finally, it may also help to try some breathing exercises or calming exercises, like going through each of the five senses and asking questions like: What do you see? What do you hear? "Once you slow down the body, it really helps that fight or flight response" that comes with anxiety, Vicksburg said.

The guidance for school during times of closure due to pandemic says that if a school continues "to provide educational opportunities to the general student population during a school closure, the school must ensure that students with disabilities also have equal access to the same opportunities."

Many districts have said they plan to continue providing meals to children. Some districts have said they will tap into online learning programs, but that presents several challenges because students don't have computers or reliable access to Wi-Fi. Because of that, some districts have said they will rely heavily on a more old-fashioned tool: learning packets. Some districts are tapping into public television to keep learning going.

Homeschooling can be overwhelming. So, first, I suggest that parents create a workable home schedule. In an effort to slow the virus's spread, almost 20 states temporarily shuttered statewide kindergarten through 12th grade schools as of Sunday, March 28. States are shifting to online instruction, just like many colleges that are ending in-person classes. News reports show that other cities and towns are taking the same approach in states that haven't yet announced closures.

Having a homeschool schedule will help because it is found to reduce stress and anxiety. As a result, I have included one for readers to use as-is, or as a beginning template to adapt into your own. A valuable homeschooling curriculum for these times can be based on the fundamental goal of teaching children at home with whatever is available. Also, a reward chart can be a very useful tool in promoting positive behavior. Teachers use it in school, and parents can use it at home.

On Monday morning, schoolchildren across the country wake up with one question: What are we doing today? Children outside of a regular school routine may suddenly be without a daily routine at all, as the coronavirus outbreak closed their schools.

As a retired educator, I am especially concerned about helping to keep children learning, and I think that one way that I can be helpful is to offer a book that presents a curriculum that includes methods of teaching children at home. This book can be used in addition to what school districts across the country are doing. It is difficult to keep students learning during closures. This book will support this challenge, making it less stressful, and more successful.

CHAPTER 1

HOMESCHOOL SCHEDULE

Creating a schedule for children helps them feel like they're taking advantage of their time off and ensures that children are still progressing academically. Using a schedule is a great way to provide structure to the day for children. It also prevents parents from heading off course.

Write the schedule out and attach it to a wall or the refrigerator to help keep children on track.

Subjects	Time	Success
Breakfast/Nutrition Study	8:00-9:00 AM	
Kitchen Math	9:00-10:00	
Home Art, Home Health Prevention	10:00-11:00	
Drop Everything and Read/ Spelling/ Writing books	11:00-12:00	
Lunch/Nutrition Study	12:00-1:00 PM	
Dramatics/ Public Speaking	1:00-2:00	
Play Time/Sleep /Rest	2:00-3:00	
Study, distance learning, google classroom, YouTube, chrome books, school assignments	3:00-4:00	
Outdoor Science / Social Studies	4:00-5:00	
Dinner	5:00-6:00	

Create a rewards chart and make a checkmark when children achieve. Small achievements that are recognized will stay with children for a long period of time because children love to look back and embrace recognition.

REWARDS CHART						
CLASSES	Week 1	Week 2	Week 3	Week 4	Week 5	Week 6
HOMESCHOOLING SCHEDULE	√					
THE PANDEMIC CRISIS						
COMPUTER SAFETY						
HOME ART						
HOME MUSIC						
DRAMATICS						
KITCHEN MATH						
BREAKFAST AND LUNCH NUTRITION						
PHYSICAL FITNESS						
SICKNESS AND HEALTH PREVENTION						
PUBLIC SPEAKING – SHOW AND TELL						
DROP EVERYTHING AND READ						
WRITING BOOKS						
SPELLING						
FAMILY WEIGHTS AND MEASURES						
SOCIAL STUDIES						
OUTDOOR SCIENCE						
READING IN THE CAR						

CHAPTER 2

DISCUSSING THE PANDEMIC VIRUS WITH CHILDREN

With the assistance of news media, distance learning, computers and other electronic devices, give students a chance to react to the effects of the pandemic in regards to the following:

1. Social distancing in the world
2. Homeschooling
3. Parents finding care for their children
4. Continuing the learning of children
5. Interruptions of lifestyles
6. Cancellation of public gatherings
7. Closing of libraries and museums
8. Parents juggling working from home
9. Stress of lost jobs such as the economy slowing
10. Limited options for getting children out of the house
11. How to avoid infections and spread the disease
12. Stopping germs and staying healthy
13. Everyday actions to reduce the spread of germs
14. Drawing pictures of the virus
15. Writing songs, raps, poems about the pandemic
16. Discussing their own personal feelings about the pandemic

CHAPTER 3

COMPUTER SAFETY

Engage children in a discussion of how to keep safe while searching for facts on the computer. Be sure to cover the potential dangers they should watch for and regular precautions they should take, such as:

1. Good decisions online—even when parents are not around.
2. Rules children should know.
3. What is expected of children while using computers or other devices.
4. Not waiting until something bad happens to start following guidelines.
5. The bad idea of posting personal information online such as phone numbers, addresses, and credit cards.

6. If criminals gain access to this information, they can use it to harm them or their family.

7. Posting only something online if comfortable with everyone in the world seeing it.

8. Avoiding the risk of eye strain, wrist strain, and other injuries by limiting the amount of time your kids spend on computers and mobile devices.

9. The chance that the internet can become an addiction and affect a person's offline life.

10. The dangers on bad websites, chat rooms, computer games, social networking sites, when accessing the Internet on mobile phones.

11. Threats online such as cyber bullies.

12. When to block messages.

13. When to contact parents or adults when receiving unwanted messages.

14. Scams, viruses, and malware to watch for.

15. Don't post anything that can harm one's reputation.

16. The value of using parental controls on the computer and electronic devices.

CHAPTER 4

HOME ART

Ask children to look throughout the house and choose something they would like to draw, construct, craft, or create. Give them the choice of using crayons, pencils, markers, play dough, straws, clay, computer, mud, paper, or any medium necessary to create artwork such as:

1. Persons, places, or things they have experienced in life
2. Things in the house they like
3. Things in the yard or neighborhood they see
4. Family members, themselves, or siblings

CHAPTER 5

MUSIC AT HOME

Using distance learning, YouTube, computers, and mobile devices give children the choice of singing or writing their own songs or raps about things such as:

1. Persons, places, or things they have experienced in life
2. Experiences
3. Things inside or outside the house
4. Holidays
5. Church
6. Stories
7. Daily life
8. Computer-generated information

CHAPTER 6

DRAMATICS

Using distance learning, computers, and mobile devices give students a chance to imitate, write, create, speak, and perform skits about:

1. Happy or sad experiences
2. Life challenges
3. Things in or around the house
4. People, plants, animals, insects
5. Things generated on electronic devices
6. Interactions with others

CHAPTER 7

KITCHEN MATH

With the use of distance learning, computers, mobile devices, and magazine and books, give children a chance to discover, examine, and name sizes and dimensions of things in the kitchen that are:

1. In the shape of circles, squares, rectangles, angles
2. Tall, short, hot, cold
3. Used for eating, baking, steaming, cooking
4. In cans, jars, or boxes
5. Fresh, canned, processed
6. Boiled, fried, steamed

CHAPTER 8

BREAKFAST AND LUNCH NUTRITION

Ask children to use distance learning, books, computers, and mobile devices to identify the following nutrients that are in foods they eat and explain how important the nutrients are to body wellness.

1. Iodine, Zinc, Copper, Chromium, Riboflavin
2. Vitamins ABCDEK, B12, B6
3. Iron, Thiamin, Niacin, Folate, Biotin
4. Sodium, Sugar, Salt
5. Potassium
6. Magnesium
7. Selenium
8. Manganese
9. Protein Fiber

CHAPTER 9

PHYSICAL FITNESS AT HOME

Tramiyah Clark

Give children, with access to computers, TV, or mobile devices, a chance to keep themselves fit by choosing to do at least one of these daily activities:

1. Walk – If the weather is nice, get outside and enjoy the scenery. Just walk around the house a few times. It may not be very exciting, but it will do the job!

2. Jumping Jacks are also great cardio exercises, and good for warming up.

3. Pushups – Do them on your knees, instead of keeping your legs straight. Or, do them standing up against a wall. You will be building up arm strength and working out muscles in your chest area.

4. Leg Lifts strengthen muscles and legs. If you find it hard to do the exercises with your legs straight, try bending them slightly.

5. Crunches are the best exercise for building up and strengthening abdominal muscles.

6. Jog in place at home while watching TV or listening to music.

7. Squats by sitting and standing up and down again from a regular chair.

8. Light Weight Lifting by using whatever you can find in your house, such as a can of peas, milk jugs, water jugs.

9. Dance – Dance to your favorite music or with YouTube. A wonderful exercise that is great for your heart.

10. Step Exercise by using the steps in the house to tone leg muscles.

CHAPTER 10

SICKNESS AND HEALTH PREVENTION AT HOME

With your assistance, distance learning, computers, and other mobile devices, give children a chance to discover and research things in the home that can make them sick such as:

1. **MOLD**
   a. Most mold in homes is a surface mold like mildew, while others can be black or green mold that will penetrate the structure of your home, making it unstable.
   b. All types of mold are irritants to respiratory systems and can cause huge problems for those with compromised immune systems. That's why it is so important to identify and remove mold from every surface of your home.

2. **PILLOWS, MATTRESSES, AND SHEETS**
   a. Pillows and mattresses that are not cleaned properly are filled with particles of the skin cells we shed and the dust mites that feed on that skin. The mites can produce a severe allergic reaction for many.
   b. <u>Sheets</u> that are not washed often can contain bacteria like Salmonella and E. coli, which can cause infections and spread illness.
3. Food Handling
   a. If food is not cooked and handled properly, there are health dangers.
   b. Improper temperatures, storage, washing, and cross-contamination are dangerous to children and anyone with compromised immune systems.
4. Kitchen
   a. Sinks, drain openings, and garbage disposals that are not cleaned regularly are a petri dish of bacteria of some type of coliform bacteria, including E. coli.
   b. It is important to use separate boards for produce and meats to avoid cross-contamination.
   c. Sponges and dishcloths can harbor Salmonella and E. coli and using them to wipe down kitchen counters simply spreads the bacteria. Proper and frequent cleaning is a must.
5. Garage
   a. An attached garage can cause problems if solvents, paints, pesticides and automotive products are stored there.
   b. Leaking or corroded containers cause the chemicals to react with the air and become less stable and more corrosive.
   c. Any opened containers should be stored in a ventilated space that is not connected to your living spaces.
   d. Carbon monoxide from fuel combustion is undetectable to the nose and is a silent killer.

e. If cars are running in the garage or tools that burn petroleum fuels are being used, keep all doors and windows open to increase airflow.

6. Cleaning Chemicals

    a. Harsh cleaning chemicals can be caustic to the skin, cause breathing issues, and are dangerous for pregnant women. The use of some chemicals, like mixing chlorine bleach and ammonia, can result in toxic fumes that can cause death very quickly.

    b. Open windows when cleaning, and use a fan to increase air-flow. Choose more natural cleaning methods that are far less toxic to humans and pets.

7. Older Building Materials

    a. Lead plumbing pipes: Lead from old pipes will leak into water systems and can cause poisoning. Children and those with compromised immune systems are most vulnerable.

    b. Vinyl flooring: In homes built before 1972, most vinyl tile flooring contains asbestos. If this flooring is cracked or you attempt to remove it, asbestos is released into the air.

8. Wall-to-Wall Carpet

    a. Wall-to-wall carpet is a bacteria and dirt magnet.

    b. For those with allergies, the dust, dust mites, and pet dander in the carpet can cause breathing issues and skin conditions.

    c. Hardwood floors with washable throw rugs produce many fewer irritants.

CHAPTER 11

PUBLIC SPEAKING – SHOW AND TELL

Di'trinae Pettis

With parent assistance, resources in the home, computers and mobile devices, give children a chance to develop presentation skills by showing and telling about subjects such as:

1. Trips
2. Animals
3. Games
4. Experiences
5. Objects
6. Things they love to do

CHAPTER 12

DROP EVERYTHING AND READ

Tramiyah Clark

With the use of distance learning, computers, and mobile devices, give children a period of the day to drop everything and read:

1. Books
2. Magazines
3. Computers and other electronic devices
4. Material written by themselves
5. Recipes
6. Documents

CHAPTER 13

WRITING BOOKS

Give children a chance to use distance learning, computers, and other mobile devices to assist them in doing the following:

1. Name the title of a book they would like to write
2. Research information about a book they would like to write
3. Write down or dictate the contents of the book to a parent or adult if they cannot write
4. Write their own book with or without assistance
5. Ask questions while they write their book
6. Look up spelling words as they write
7. Read their book to a sibling or family member

CHAPTER 14

SPELLING THINGS IN THE HOME

Give children access to computers or other mobile devices to aid them in spelling and pronouncing things in the home such as:

1. Kitchen utensils
2. Foods
3. Equipment
4. Lights
5. Shades
6. Curtains
7. Doors
8. Windows
9. Furniture
10. Dishes
11. Glassware

CHAPTER 15

FAMILY WEIGHTS AND MEASURES

Give children access to scales, mobile devices, yard sticks, rulers, instruments, and tapes, to help them compare, record, and do family member measurements such as:

1. Height
2. Weight
3. Waist size
4. Head size
5. Length of the right arm
6. Compare measurements of their family members

CHAPTER 16

SOCIAL STUDIES

Using computers, books, and devices, give children a chance to identify, draw, paint, explain, discuss, or sing about the following symbols, landmarks, monuments, holidays, historical figures, government facts, and cultural celebrations.

1. American symbols, landmarks, and monuments
    a. The American flag
    b. The White House
    c. The Washington Monument
    d. The Lincoln Memorial
    e. The Statue of Liberty
    f. The Empire State Building
2. The Golden Gate Bridge
    a. Mount Rushmore
3. Historical figures

a. Benjamin Franklin

b. Paul Revere

c. Thomas Jefferson

d. Davy Crockett

e. John Deere

f. Abraham Lincoln

g. Frederick Douglass

h. Susan B. Anthony

i. Harriet Tubman

j. Sitting Bull

k. Thomas Edison

l. Theodore Roosevelt

m. George Washington Carver

n. Amelia Earhart

o. Thurgood Marshall

p. Rosa Parks

q. Jackie Robinson

r. Cesar Chavez

s. Martin Luther King, Jr.

t. Neil Armstrong

u. Bill Gates

4. Government

a. Purpose of government

b. Local government

c. State government

d. Federal government

e. The Constitution

f. The Bill of Rights

g. Checks and balances

h. Presidential elections

5. Cultural celebrations

a. Thanksgiving

b. Hanukkah

c. Rosh Hashanah

d. Kwanzaa

e. Christmas

f. Easter

g. Lunar New Year

h. Ramadan

i. Día de los Muertos

CHAPTER 17

OUTDOOR SCIENCE

With the assistance of TV, mobile devices, or books, ask children to define different types of weather conditions such as:

1. Sunny
2. Cloudy
3. Rainy
4. Stormy

Give children the opportunity to listen to weather reports on TV or mobile devices and do the following:

1. Sing about weather
2. Write about weather conditions

3. Draw pictures of different types of weather

4. Create their own weather report and give it orally

Ask children to collect snow in a container and answer the following questions:

1. Is it warm or cold?
2. Does it melt?
3. Where does it come from?
4. Can it be eaten?
5. Why do we need snow?
6. Is it a gas, liquid, or solid?

Give students the opportunity to discover and research things out-of-doors by:

1. Taking pictures of insects, worms, birds, or animals. Show and tell about them.
2. Using books, magazines, or mobile devices to find and study more information about these creatures, explain and write down what is found.

Give children a chance to catch rain in a bowl or cup, examine it, and answer the following questions.

1. How is it made?
2. How does it fall from the sky?
3. Why is it needed? Is it a liquid, a gas, or a solid?

Ask children to look at the sun and answer the following questions:

1. What is it made of?
2. How far is it from the earth? Why is it needed?
3. Is it a liquid, a gas, or a solid?

CHAPTER 18

READING LESSONS IN THE CAR

Ask children to use mobile devices to read and take photographs of what they see as they ride in the car.

1. Explain to children that they will make a book about their neighborhood signs.
2. Ask children to sort the pictures into categories (business signs, safety signs, public notices, and so on).
3. Involve children in organizing the photographs, mounting them and writing about what they see and read. They should include the drawings and dictations that they created during their ride.
4. Encourage children to identify signs that they already know.
5. Point out the different types of lettering, lighting, or pictures that are used to make signs.
   a. Safety signs

b. Traffic signs

c. Business signs

d. Public notices

e. Building signs

f. Different types of road signs

g. Words on buildings

h. Words on street signs

i. Instructions

j. Shapes they see

k. Construction signs

l. Signs with pictures

m. Places where they see signs

n. Different shapes of signs

o. Different places where they see signs

p. Draw and write about their trip

CHAPTER 19

GROCERY STORE MATH

Give children a chance to use distance learning, computers, and mobile devices to help them to practice using money, budgeting, identifying food groups, and practice reading and writing grocery store items by doing the following:

1. **Make a Picture List (Ages 2–4)**

    Give children the latest grocery circular, a pair of safety scissors, some glue and paper. Then, read off a grocery store list one item at a time, asking children to find a picture of that item. Have children cut it out and glue it to the paper. Repeat with as many items on your list as you think the children can handle. When children are finished, their pictures should match the list.

2. **Write the List**

   Give children a pencil and a piece of paper. Name off what you need to buy at the store and ask them to write those items down.

3. **Colors**

   Challenge your child to find a number of different items that match the colors in a basic 8-pack of crayons (red, blue, yellow, green, orange, black, brown, purple). Older children can be challenged to find more unusual and hard-to-find colors such as magenta.

4. **Food Groups**

   Discuss with the children different food groups needed to build a healthy meal. Once your child has a good sense of what foods fall into each group, ask the child to identify sections of the store designed for fruits, vegetables, grains, and protein.

   Ask children to find, write, and/or draw four of each type of food.

CHAPTER 20

HEALTH IN THE BATHROOM

Ask students to go to the internet at http://abcnews.go.com/Health/Wellness/10-health-hazards-lurking-bathroom. Have them study, and then collect data about:

Slips and falls in the bathroom that can pose a serious health hazard.

How to safeguard themselves against potentially disastrous falls. So alongside vigilance, the use of rubber mats, padding of protruding objects, and adding handles to areas where slippage is likely — like the wall alongside the shower — are just some simple ways to prevent such accidents from occurring.

Cotton swabs

Cotton swabs can damage the ear, and rupture ear drums.

Just don't use them!

Swabs can introduce bacteria into the ear, which then causes infection.

Mold

Showers provide the ideal environment for mold to develop. This can cause real problems for people with respiratory problems like asthma, as well as giving your bathroom walls a gruesome makeover.

The kind of mold found in homes that can bring about asthma is called stachybotrys — a black, sticky, slimy fungus. Nevertheless, not being able to see it doesn't necessarily mean it's not there. In the right environment, mold spores can grow within 48 hours. Symptoms of exposure to this kind of mold include nausea, recurring headaches, and asthma-like symptoms.

You can also run an exhaust fan both while washing and for a further 20 minutes after that.

No moisture = no mold. So remember: ventilate, ventilate, ventilate!

Scented shampoo

There is a much greater understanding now than there used to be about the potentially harmful substances in some shampoo bottles. A report released in March 2009, for example, highlighted the frequent use of the chemicals formaldehyde and 1,4-dioxane in hair products, both of which have been linked to cancer and a number of skin conditions.

Generally, the main purpose of such additions is to prolong the life of the product. However, it's clear that a greater effort needs to be made to eradicate these substances from use in cosmetics. It's clear that some improvements have been made, particularly with the recent surge in popularity of the natural products industry. So, whenever you change shampoo, always check what it says on the bottle.

Splash!

Despite what many might think, in general the toilet is a shining example of cleanliness, due to the fact that most toilets are regularly disinfected. It is what the toilet projects onto the world around it that we are concerned about here.

Every time you flush, a spray of water droplets is produced. Contained within these droplets are bacteria that generate E. coli. When the lid is left up during the flush, such bacteria will be dispersed onto anything within close proximity, such as toothbrushes, hand towels, and bars of soap. Not a nice thought.

In this case, the solution couldn't be simpler: put a lid on it! By the way, do you know the most dangerous thing in the house? You often come into contact with it after leaving the bathroom… it's a pair of trousers. They cause more accidents than anything else. Always put your trousers on while sitting on something, not standing up!

CHAPTER 21

STEPPING UP AFTER UNPRECEDENTED CLOSING OF SCHOOLS

I am writing this book as my way of stepping up and making a contribution to helping parents, students, and teachers during the sudden, unprecedented changes brought about in response to coronavirus and the closing of schools. I wanted to step up and be a leader during these challenging times because I am a retired educator who feels that it is my duty to do whatever I can to address educational issues.

I have found that being of service to others is a positive way to counter the anxiety and negativity heard throughout the country. So, consider how you can step up and be a leader.

We must not forget the anxiety and frustration students and parents feel about the pandemic and school closings. What can we do to find solutions and extend or locate support?

A CBS news article published March 16, 2020 said that parents and students nationwide contend with school closures with "overwhelming anxiety."

"This is the new normal for so many parents across the country," said CBS News correspondent Meg Oliver, reporting from her house in Montclair, New Jersey, where her children are also home from school, logging onto their computers for online classes.

And as more schools shut down, the inability of many families to afford laptops for their children is a huge problem.

Olivia Austin is an eighth-grade social studies teacher in Newark, New Jersey, where schools are closed throughout the state. "I feel bad because I don't have any answers right now, either," she said via Skype. "Schools offer a type of security that they thrive off of, so just not having that sense of security is also an added stress."

Austin is concerned that her students could fall behind on their curriculum.

"One of the biggest challenges is, I work in an inner-city school, and a lot of our students don't have access to laptops."

Another concern at the top of educators' minds: providing meals to students who rely on school lunches as their primary source of nutrition.

In Virginia, the Arlington public school system started a "grab and go" initiative, where students will be able to pick up breakfast and lunch bags while schools remain out of session for the next four weeks.

"About 30% of our students in Arlington participate in the free and reduced meals program," said Amy Maclosky, food services director for Arlington Public Schools. "So, I do think that there would be students who had nothing to eat tomorrow for breakfast."

Kristin Little is a single mom with two kids who are expected to be at home for the next month at a minimum. "We need more than 12–24 hours to plan for the complete disruption of, not just our lives, but the lives of children," she said.

"My first reaction when I got the notification, they were going to shutter the schools for a month was instant, overwhelming anxiety, and I broke into tears," she said. "Because you're just completely not mentally or physically prepared for something like that."

News reports of the expressions that teachers voiced show that it is a loss to not get to have that chance to say goodbye to students. "It is a different connection when you are teaching a five-year-old and you feel like they are your own," said Fisher.

Fisher said the move is for the best. Meantime, she is trying to find ways to keep her younger students engaged as she tests out online learning.

"As I was watching the screen, the longer it went on, the more I could see some of the kids losing interest, and getting up and leaving, and coming back, and running around in a room," said Fisher.

Many parents can relate to Erica Petrowski, who is now taking on the role of teacher. With four children at home, her new job isn't easy.

"It has been challenging for me personally, because it has caused me anxiety," said Petrowski.

Tempe Union High School District started online classes today. But for some, access to online resources isn't even possible.

"It is a little confusing for a lot of students. A lot of them don't have computers at home. They are using their cell phones primarily to do the work," said Steve Adams, a visual arts teacher at Mountain Pointe High School.

Adams said the district handed out thousands of computers to students in need, but they couldn't provide them for everyone. District officials said this is one of their biggest concerns, and they are working on ways to get everyone the resources they need.

Let some of these many examples of giving back inspire you to help parents, teachers, students, and others in times of school closings and a pandemic.

President Elizabeth A. Davis of the Washington Teachers Union Stepped up.

Under the direction of WTU President Elizabeth Davis, WTU is partnering with Fox5, its sister station, Fox Plus WDCA-TV, and ABC to air lessons on television for students during school closures.

The WTU continues to monitor updates from local and national experts concerning the spread of COVID-19.

Broadcast: Fox Plus, WDCA-TV, Weekdays at 10 a.m.

Each day of the week will feature a 30-minute lesson for a particular grade group. Mondays will be for early childhood learners and 1st graders; Tuesdays will be for 2nd and 3rd graders; Wednesdays for

4th and 5th graders; Thursdays for 6th, 7th and 8th graders; and Fridays for 9th through 12th graders.

The WTU's Professional Development Director, Sarah Elwell, hosted teachers for a chat to present information to prepare for distance learning. You can access her presentation here or contact her at selwell@wtulocal6.net with your questions.

The American Federation of Teachers (AFT) stepped up by providing useful and regularly updated guidance for how teachers, school staff, and local K-12 leaders can prepare for the coronavirus. Learn more here: https://aflcio.org/covid-

Individuals and families can learn more about <u>How to be Prepared</u> here: <u>bit.ly/3cvprep</u>

DCPS prepared instructional distance learning contingency plans to allow meaningful, relevant learning to take place while schools are closed. They developed resources for every level in grades PK-8 and each graduation requirement course for grades 9-12. Information about how to pick up printed copies of the lessons throughout the city or access them online was shared in the news and online

Also, free meals for students were made available to students on weekdays daily from 10:00 a.m. to 2:00 p.m. at various sites.

Mayor of the District of Columbia, Muriel Bowser, stepped up by declaring both a state of emergency and a public health emergency. During this unprecedented public health emergency, DC Public Schools (DCPS) remains committed to ensuring the well-being of students and school communities. **Therefore, starting Monday, March 16 through Tuesday, March 31, DCPS will modify operations to help mitigate the spread of coronavirus (COVID-19) in our region.**

In efforts to address community health risks and ensure the continuity of learning for our students, DCPS was ordered to follow an updated schedule between March 16 and March 31:

1. *Monday, March 16* — Teachers and staff will report to school to plan for distance learning. No school for students.
2. *Tuesday, March 17 to Monday, March 23* — DCPS will take its Spring Break for students and teachers. There will no longer be a Spring Break period in April.
3. *Tuesday, March 24 to Tuesday, March 31* — Students will participate in distance learning.
4. *Wednesday, April 1* — Schools will resume operations.

During this period, there will also be no school-sponsored activities such as athletics, extracurriculars, field trips, events, or after-school programs.

We are grateful for the patience, flexibility, and cooperation our DCPS community is demonstrating as we manage the dynamic nature of this event. As we approach the next few weeks, we ask for continued patience and trust as the District navigates this unique situation. While this decision was made to prioritize the health and safety of our entire school community, we understand it will be disruptive to our families. With that in mind, I want to share some additional details about what distance learning will look like for our DCPS students and the supports we have in place for families over the next few weeks.

Microsoft is offering anyone its premium version of Teams for free for six months and has lifted existing user limits on its free version. The premium Teams product was already available for no extra cost to those who pay for the Office Suite, and Teams had already been free for many schools.

Similarly, Google announced last week that it would offer its enterprise videoconferencing features — for example, larger meetings of up to 250 people and the ability to record — for free to G Suite and G Suite for Education customers through July 1, 2020.

Slack has always had a free version. Lately, it has been trying to get the influx of new users up to speed quickly by offering free webinars with live Q&As, consultations by phone, and information on working-from-home best practices.

"Given that Microsoft and Google have both enabled free use of their premium conferencing and collaboration apps, Microsoft Teams and Google's Hangouts Meet, these could be good tools for businesses that haven't ordinarily paid for these services," Lexi Sydow, senior market insights manager at App Annie, told Recode.

The *LA Times* stepped up by listing eleven television shows that can help get you and your kids through the quarantine:

1. "Ask the Storybots" (Netflix)
2. "Xavier Riddle and the Secret Museum" (PBS Kids app, PBS Kids channel on Amazon Prime Video)
3. "The Who Was? Show" (Netflix)
4. "Molly of Denali" (PBS Kids app, PBS Kids channel on Amazon Prime Video)
5. "Octonauts" (Netflix)
6. "Odd Squad" (PBS Kids app, PBS Kids channel on Amazon Prime Video)
7. "Pee-wee's Playhouse" (Netflix)
8. "Beat Bugs" (Netflix)
9. "Motown Magic" (Netflix)
10. "Too Cute" (Hulu)
11. "Creative Galaxy" (Amazon Prime Video)

The *New York Times* has also compiled a list of shows parents can "tolerate" watching with their kids.

1. "Booba" (Netflix)
2. "Puffin Rock" (Netflix)
3. "Teen Titans Go!" (Hulu, Cartoon Network)
4. "Powerpuff Girls" (Hulu, Cartoon Network)

5. "Diners, Drive-ins and Dives" (Hulu, Amazon Prime, the Food Network)

Microsoft, Google, and Zoom are trying to keep up with demand for their now free work-from-home software. As companies and schools move to online work, workplace software is put to the test.

NASP reported:

1. Responding to COVID-19: Immediate Action Steps for School Crisis Response Teams: https://www.nasponline.org/resources-and-publications/resources-and-podcasts/school-climate-safety-and-crisis/health-crises/responding-to-covid-19brief-action-steps-for-school-crisis-response-teams

2. Preparing for Infectious Disease Epidemics: Brief Tips for School Mental Health Professionals https://www.nasponline.org/resources-and-publications/resources-and-podcasts/school-climate-safety-and-crisis/health-crises/preparing-for-infectious-disease-epidemics-brief-tips-for-school-mental-health-professionals

3. Talking to Children About COVID-19 (Coronavirus): A Parent Resource https://www.nasponline.org/resources-and-publications/resources-and-podcasts/school-climate-safety-and-crisis/health-crises/talking-to-children-about-covid-19-(coronavirus)-a-parent-resource

The Federal Government stepped up with the following information:

1. Interim Guidance for Administrators of U.S. Childcare Programs and K-12 Schools to Plan, Prepare, and Respond to Coronavirus Disease 2019 (COVID-19): https://www.cdc.gov/coronavirus/2019-ncov/specific-groups/guidance-for-schools.html

2. General information on pandemic flu: HTTPs

3. Get Your School Ready for Pandemic Flu: https://www.cdc.gov/nonpharmaceutical-interventions/pdf/gr-pan-flu-ed-set.pdf

4. How to Disinfect Schools to Prevent the Spread of Flu: https://rems.ed.gov/Docs/How_to_Clean_and_Disinfect_Schools_to_help_Slow_the_Spread_of_the_Flu.pdf

1. Handwashing and Hand Sanitizer Use at Home, at Play, and Out and About: https://www.cdc.gov/handwashing/pdf/hand-sanitizer-factsheet.pdf
2. How to cope with stress during disease outbreaks: https://store.samhsa.gov/system/files/sma14-4885.pdf
3. A Spanish version can be found at https://store.samhsa.gov/system/files/sma14-4885spanish.pdf
4. How parents can help families cope with a Pandemic Flu: https://www.nctsn.org/sites/default/files/resources/pdf

Emergency and Crisis Preparedness was revealed.

1. Guide for Developing High-Quality School Emergency Operations Plans, https://rems.ed.gov/docs/REMS_K-12_Guide_508.pdf
2. NASP's prepare School Safety and Crisis Training Curriculum, https://www.nasponline.org/3rd-edition-info

For more information related to schools and physical and mental health, visit www.nasponline.org and www.nasn.org

National Association of School Psychologists. (2020). Reported. Preparing for a Pandemic Illness: Guidelines for School Administrators and Crisis Teams

Here are almost 50 examples of companies doing good for the world during this coronavirus pandemic:

1. Microsoft announced that they will keep paying the hourly workers who support their campus.

2. Google established a COVID-19 fund that enables all temporary staff and vendors, globally, to take paid sick leave if they have potential symptoms of COVID-19, or can't come into work because they're quarantined. They have also made their video-conferencing service, Hangouts Meet, available for all G-suite customers until July 1, 2020.

3. Loom, a video recording and sharing service has made Loom Pro free for teachers and students at K-12 schools, universities, and educational institutions. They have also removed the recording limit on free plans and have cut the price for Loom Pro in half.

4. Mark Cuban announced that any of his employees (including those who work for the Mavericks) will be reimbursed for any lunch and coffee purchases from local, independent small businesses.

5. Forbes hosted on March 20, 2020 on the theme of Business Resilience: Thriving in Crucial Times. The speaker roster included top experts and best-selling authors such as Chris Brogan, Rohit Bhargava, and Dorie Clark. Many of the speakers were slated to speak at the cancelled SXSW this year.

6. Shine Distillery in Portland started making and giving away hand sanitizer in an acute shortage.

7. The Barbara Bush Foundation for Family Literacy's in-house team of literacy and education experts has created a toolkit of high-quality online resources that can be used anytime, anywhere, helping parents navigate the vast amount of available options.

8. LinkedIn is opening up 16 of its learning courses for free. Courses that provide tips on how to stay productive, build relationships when you're not face-to-face, use virtual meeting tools and balance family and work dynamics in a healthy way.

9. Jamm, an audio-visual communication tool used by remote and distributed teams, is offering its service free of charge.

10. Adobe is giving higher education and K-12 institutional customers of their Creative Cloud apps the ability to request temporary "at-home" access for their students and educators. This is being granted through May 31, 2020 at no additional cost and is available globally.

11. Meero, a file transfer service, is offering free large-file transfers to ease remote working.

12. OneDine is offering a free Tap & Pay Touchless Payment system to restaurants during the COVID-19 crisis.

13. Amazon is hiring 100,000 more workers and giving raises to current staff to deal with coronavirus demands.

14. Chef José Andrés of LA set up shop in California earlier this month to feed cruise ship guests quarantined from the outbreak. Andrés announced this week he will transform eight of his New York and Washington, DC, restaurants into community kitchens for those struggling during the pandemic.

15. Sweetgreen has announced it will start dedicating Outpost operations and teams to support "those on the front lines" (meaning hospital workers and medical personnel) by delivering free salads and bowls to hospitals in the cities it serves.

16. Pizza's CEO Michael Lastoria notified employees last week that the company is offering free, unlimited pizzas to front-line workers and their immediate families, as well as to hospital workers who show identification. The company is also raising hourly pay by $1 and 14 days of "health and safety pay" to employees who have tested positive or who have come in contact with someone with coronavirus.

17. Everytable, a Los Angeles–based café, launched a helpline to ensure that everyone in its market has access to healthy meals during this time.

18. Starbucks has extended its mental health benefits. In partnership with Lyra Health, Starbucks is offering its partners personalized, confidential mental health care, 20 free in-person or video sessions every year for partners and each of their eligible family members, online scheduling with most providers available within two weeks, and access to a provider network of mental health therapists and coaches.

19. UberEats and DoorDash have waived commission fees for independent restaurant partners, while Postmates has launched a pilot program for small businesses that temporarily waives commission fees for businesses in the SF Bay Area.

20. Dolce & Gabbana announced that it has partnered with Humanities University to fund a coronavirus research project.

21. Giorgio Armani has donated $1.43 million to four hospitals in Rome and Milan, as well as to the Civil Protection Agency.

22. French luxury group Kering, which owns brands like Gucci and Bottega Veneta, has donated 2 million euros to help the fight against the coronavirus outbreak.

23. Miuccia Prada and Patrizio Bertelli, the CEO of Prada, came to the region's aid by donating two full intensive care and resuscitation units each to three Milanese hospitals.

24. Alphabet (Google's parent company) created a COVID-19 fund to provide sick leave to affected workers globally, including all temporary staff, contractors, and vendors.

25. Amazon just announced that it will offer unlimited paid sick leave over the next month, but only for those who test positive for COVID-19.

26. Apple is now offering its retail staff unlimited paid sick leave to anyone experiencing coronavirus symptoms.

27. Darden Restaurants (Olive Garden, Longhorn Steakhouse, others) has announced paid sick leave for all of its hourly workers not currently covered by a corporate policy.

28. McDonald's has stated that it will cover sick leave for any employees at corporate-owned locations who are asked to quarantine for two weeks.

29. Walmart has deployed an Emergency Leave program, which provides time-off for employees depending on various coronavirus threat levels.

30. Uber announced they will provide 14 days of sick pay for drivers or delivery workers – technically considered independent contractors who have not previously qualified for paid leave or benefits – who are sick with the coronavirus or are required to be isolated.

31. Amazon created a $25M fund to help its delivery drivers and seasonal workers cope with coronavirus, and a $5M dollar fund to help affected small businesses in Seattle.

32. Amazon and Microsoft have each pledged $2.5 million, with the possibility of more, to help out those afflicted by the disease in Seattle.

33. According to Business Insider. Com,Comcast, Charter, Verizon, Google, T-Mobile, and Sprint and dozens of other internet and phone providers have signed an FCC pledge to keep American internet-connected for the next 60 days, even if people cannot afford to pay during disruptions caused by the Coronavirus.

49. NBCUniversal is now offering its newest movies including *The Hunt* and *The Invisible Man* for affordable rates on demand.

Let these examples of giving back inspire you to see how you can help people in your community, or in your business. Helping and being of service to others is a positive way to counter the anxiety and negativity swirling around in the media constantly. Look around and consider how you can step up and be a leader during this challenging time for the world.

A list was published addressing "quarantine, school closures, weekend social distancing, or anytime," according to the list's makers:

1. Have each child pick a topic they'd like to learn about and spend 30 minutes each day on that topic.
2. Spend one day reading every single picture book in the house.
3. Go through all the old mail laying around (ok, that one's not for kids, although they do enjoy helping tear stuff up).
4. Bake something every day.
5. Have each kid write a letter and/or emails to a different friend or family member each day.
6. Use all of your building toys on one giant structure.

7. Wash your hands!!!!

8. Races of various kinds in the backyard (hopping on one foot, crabwalk, walking backward, etc.).

9. Try stop motion animation with playdough.

10. Facetime grandparents a lot.

11. Watch everything on Disney+.

12. Inventory the plants & wildlife (from bugs on up) in your yard.

13. Learn the parts of plants/flowers & how they function (bonus if they learn the Latin names).

14. If you aren't too squeamish & have a spare clear shoebox-size tote or 5-10 gallon tank, catch some pillbugs (rolly pollies, sowbugs) & observe them.

15. Write a short story & illustrate it.

16. Learn how to do simple bookbinding.

17. Make paper (from your old mail).

18. Have the kids help with yard work in between playing games outside. They're little, but they like getting dirty and "working" in the gardens.

19. GoNoodle! Great for guided movement, relaxation, etc.

20. Board games, card games.

21. Legos.

22. We have some extreme dot to dot books (1400 dots) that the kids love, especially the 5-year-old!

23. Lots of reading, playing with the dog.

24. Working on learning to sew using stuff on hand.

25. Card making/scrapbooking projects.

26. Getting the garden ready.

27. Make tents and reading caves: flashlights, tidy snacks, books, and pillows!

28. Have a shadow show in the reading tent (use blankets over chairs or a table).

29. Get binoculars and learn about the birds near your house. Look them up on Google and search for their birdcalls on YouTube.

30. Learn how to make a stuffed animal.

31. Play with cornstarch and water and cheap action figures.

32. Many educational websites are waving fees if your student's school is closed. Here's a list of all of them that are waving fees.

33. Collect a bunch of tape, markers, and cardboard boxes. That'll keep them busy for a day or two.

34. Watch all the handwashing videos & vote on your favorite. Discuss why each is good, helpful, or funny. The Holderness parody one is hilarious, the Vietnam Tiktok one is great choreography, some have good songs, etc.

35. Also, pick your favorite song with a 20-second refrain or verse perfect for handwashing length of time.

36. Family puzzles. Ones that are 500–1000 pieces and are challenging but not frustrating.

37. We homeschool (4 kids) and honestly, just have fun!!!!!

38. Team up and really clean and organize each kid's space, making a donation box for each. Parents are included.

39. Have a board game day.

40. Kids can also make their own games! Board games, card games, you name it!

41. Write a story cooperatively. One person picks a character, and the other picks a setting, and then go gangbusters together.

42. The folding picture story one! Called "eat poop you cat." One person draws a small picture across the top of a paper; the next person writes a sentence that describes that picture and folds over the top of the paper hot dog style to cover the picture. So the 3rd person only sees a sentence and they have to draw a picture. They fold over the sentence.

43. Any and all art is fun at home: beading, painting, drawing, play-dough or kinetic sand, sewing, etc.

44. Massive board game tournament with all the (mostly forgotten) board games you own!

45. If your school is going on quarantine and running school online, get Global Kids for the special price of just $10.98. Take a screen-free, curiosity + creativity boosting, global empathy + engagement trip around the world, from the comfort of your home.

46. My daughter (6) has enjoyed doing yoga at home. There are kid-friendly YouTube videos and printed cards with poses.

47. Zumba or dance-along videos on YouTube.

48. We homeschool exclusively and the best advice I have is checking out Pinterest. There are tons of ideas for activities, games, etc.

49. Draw self-portraits on blank faces.

50. Color-code different interesting places on a map.

51. Draw maps of places, and then make directions from one place to another to see if someone else could follow it.

52. Scavenger hunts, indoor treasure hunts, where they follow clues through the house to a "treasure" at the end (could be candy, a movie, whatever), and a lot of charades.

53. I made videos with my 3rd-grade daughter teaching kids how to write code. Check out the videos here.

54. My daughter wanted a dollhouse for her 18" dolls. We saved cardboard boxes and got more from Dollar General and got to work. The closets and couch are cardboard as well.

55. There are a few easy "kitchen chemistry" type science experiments that are easy to do, like making slime, baking soda and vinegar reaction, etc.

56. We put food coloring under the baking soda in a mini muffin pan and used a pipette to drop vinegar in, and then we can see the color!

57. Last summer we did an experiment to learn what each ingredient did for a cake (so we made one following the recipe, one without

eggs, one without milk, etc.). We then compared and contrasted different cakes. Then we ate a lot of weird cake.

58. There are a bunch of ideas on the lab section of this website. And we have letters from women in STEM around the world!

59. Give the dogs a bath and brush.

60. Wash and clean out my car (mostly their food trash and dirty socks).

61. Mow the lawn (my 11 year old just learned!).

62. Play sidewalk chalk outside.

63. Glow stick party.

64. Popcorn + movie marathon.

65. Listen to kid podcasts.

66. Declutter toys!

67. Have an Olympics with a bunch of events competitions: funny ones, helpful ones (like cleaning) and really fun ones (like minute to win it style).

68. Learn new card games.

69. We're going to learn to make sushi!

70. Lots of art projects!

71. Dig up all the activity books, presents, etc. that never got played with, and use those!

72. There's always the time-tested building a tent in the house with blankets and chairs. Great for just before nap time.

73. We are going to bust out our hiking gear and try new hiking paths. As long as you stay away from overpopulated areas, you will naturally stay a safe distance from others and sick people generally don't hike!

74. Do a study on planets, then have the kids create their own planets. How big is it, where in the universe is it located, atmosphere conditions, can it sustain life, how long is a day/year, name it, etc. You could even spread the planets out around the house to show

approximate distance from each other. <u>Watch this to learn about relative distance.</u>

75. Design a new spacecraft, draw plans, then create out of Legos or household items. Spend some time pretending you're on different planets with different gravity, you could seriously spend a whole week on just fun space activities.

76. But that's not limited to space. These ideas would work for animals, geography, body systems, historical events/time periods, etc. Beyond that, do some fun physics experiments like making a bridge out of straws, egg drop protectors, paper airplanes, etc.

77. Puppet Master: an app where you can animate anything from a drawing to a stuffed animal.

78. Practice spinning poi. My daughter is just learning how to spin and it's been fun practicing together.

79. Puzzle races: Put several puzzles (20+ piece puzzles) in a paper bag and shake it up. Pour pieces out and give each person the puzzle box they are to put together. Go!

80. Dig through cabinets and figure out recipes for that thing you got at the grocery store and thought "this is interesting…surely it can be used for something!" And then make it.

It is my hope that the information in this book, including the many examples of giving back, will educate and inspire others to help parents, students, and teachers during sudden, unprecedented times.

REFERENCES AND RESOURCES

News about How Teachers Are Coping with Pandemic.

bing.com/news

How are Catholics coping with school closures?

Washington D.C., Mar 17, 2020 / 03:00 pm (CNA). The coronavirus pandemic has caused Catholic …

Catholic News Agency · 13d

How Did LA Cope With The Influenza Pandemic Of 1918?

LAist · 5d

Life Across America During the Coronavirus Pandemic: Stories About How You Are Coping

What are your concerns and how is your community coping? More than 2,000 of you responded … I'm …

NBC DFW · 3d

'You almost feel stuck': How parents are coping with kids doing schoolwork at home

Buffalo News · 12d

'I feel a lot of anxiety': How residents are coping with coronavirus

The Clarion-Ledger (… · 8d

'I miss school': How students are coping with remote learning during …

QS · 6d

How Are Parents, Students, And Teachers Dealing With School Closures?

KALW · 4d

How international students are coping with the coronavirus lockdown in …

Copenhagen Post · 10h

How are you dealing with social distancing? Share your stories with us

Grand Haven Tribune · 13d

How Teachers Can Stay Balanced During the Pandemic | Teach ...

https://www.teachforamerica.org/stories/how...

10 days ago ·

How Teachers Can Stay Balanced During the **Pandemic** ... **Teachers** across the country have been faced with the daunting and heroic task of radically revising their plans and designing send-home and online lessons while **dealing** with their own anxieties around COVID-19. We spoke with clinical psychologist Dr. Richard Shadick, who is Teach For ...

YouTube › Jill Plummer

Mar 16, 2020 · You're **welcome, Liz.** The **REAL heroes** in this are the teachers, **SLPs,** and **others who developed these materials and are freely sharing** them. I'm **continually impressed by the generous spirit of AAC folks!**

12 days ago · Home / **Coping** with COVID-19 Our hearts go out to all who have been infected by COVID-19 and those whose lives have been disrupted by this **pandemic.** We are particularly concerned about the significant impacts this public health crisis is likely to have on our nation's child care and early learning programs, including educators, families, and ...year 12 student **dealing** with the **pandemic** ... "The State School **Teachers** Union

of Western Australia has called for the release of detailed medical advice behind the decision to keep schools and TAFEs open for the time-being.

10 Ways to Help Students Who Struggle With Anxiety

https://www.weareteachers.com/7-ways-to-help...

Oct 01, 2019 · 10 Ways to Help Students Who Struggle With Anxiety. Breathe in. Breathe out. Karen Nelson on October 1 ... kids can learn to slow down their anxious brains, and **teachers** can learn to help them. Here are a few ways you can help anxious kids in the classroom. ... and this is a great option to offer if you have students **dealing** with anxiety ...

Economic Tsunami': How the World Is Dealing With Pandemic

New Hampshire Pu... · 12d

Coronavirus Quarantine: How Are Catholics Coping with School Closures?

Coping with Stress During a Pandemic | Time Out For Teachers

https://timeoutforteachers.com/coping-with-stress-during-a-pandemic

Mar 16, 2020 · **Teachers** have added concerns With the added concerns about how to best serve students, worry for students whose main security comes from schools that are

Things in Your Home That Are Making You Sick

https://www.thespruce.com/home-objects-making-ill-4172353

National Association for Geoscience Teachers (NAGT) guides for Teaching in the Field and Safety in the Field

Special Issue of Journal of Geoscience Education on Teaching in the Field

Searchable collection of references and resources on field-based learning *from the Synthesis of Research on Learning in the Geosciences by the* Science Education Resource Center

"Field Notes" by David W. Mogk, Dept. of Earth Sciences, Montana State University: Research based methods for successful field trips, including specific examples for a geoscience course

The Out-of-Classroom Experience by Dave Douglass: A comprehensive article on things to consider when "dreaming-up, organizing, planning and leading field trips and other learning activities that will take place outside of the traditional classroom setting"

http://abcnews.go.com/Health/MindMoodNews/story?id=8053784&page=3

shelf/story? id=17728889

http://safecosmetics.org/downloads/NoMoreToxicTub_Mar09Report.pdf

——

Haisman DR, Clarke MW: Interfacial factor in heat-induced conversion of chlorophyll to pheophytin in green leaves. J Sci Food Agric. 1975, 26: 1111-1126. 10.1002/jsfa.2740260809.

Barham P: The Science of Cooking. 2000, Springer, Berlin

Flores AA, Goff HD: Ice crystal size distributions in dynamically frozen model solutions and ice cream as affected by stabilizers. J Dairy Sci. 1999, 82: 1399-1407. 10.3168/jds. S0022-0302(99)75366-X.

Faydi E, Andrieu J, Laurent P: Experimental study and modelling of the ice crystal morphology of model standard ice cream, Part I: Direct characterization method and experimental data. J Food Eng. 2001, 48: 283-291. 10.1016/S0260-8774(00)00168-0.

Google ScholarH H Wills Physics Laboratory, University of Bristol Tyndall Avenue, Bristol, BS8 1TL, UK Peter Barham

Grocery Store Learning Activities for Kids By Amanda Morin Updated on August 15, 2019

March 13, 2020

Facebook

Twitter

Email

Print

More than 100 school districts across the state, including Los Angeles Unified, have announced campus closures due to the coronavirus and parents now face a daunting task.

Bless Patawaran, left, and Cody Holmes, both 13, student leaders at Burroughs Middle School in Los Angeles, make a video demonstrating proper hand-washing technique.

(Francine Orr / Los Angeles Times) by paloma esquivel, howard blume, sonali kohli

Therapist Jonathan Vickburg, the mental health supervisor with Cedars-Sinai's Share and Care program.

ABOUT THE AUTHOR

Christine Davis Easterling

Christine Davis Easterling is an active member of First Baptist Church in Northwest Washington. At First Baptist, she serves as a member of the Board of Christian Education, director of Vacation Bible School, and chairperson of the Fall and Spring institutes. She's been a member of the First Baptist Gospel Choir for fifteen years. She teaches a Miracles of Jesus class for the Baptist Congress of Christian Education, Maryland, from her book titled *The Miracles of Jesus*. Additionally, Christine is a former Vice Principal of the District of Columbia Public Schools, and former Director of The Teaching Professions Academy.

In the 1958 class of Luther H. Foster High School she was an honor roll student, basketball player, cheerleader, member of the Dramatics Club, choir, and Parliamentarian of the Senior Class. After graduating from Luther H. Foster High, she attended Saint Paul's Episcopal College where she was an honor roll student, member of the Dramatics Guild, and was inducted into Alpha Kappa Alpha Sorority, Incorporated. She went on to earn a Master of Arts Degree from The University of D. C. and a Master's of Arts Degree from Howard University in Public School Administration.

She is the author of several books: *A Giant for Justice: Inspirational Biography of William H. "Bill" Simons III*, which is a twenty-five-year history of the Washington Teachers' Union, and *The Miracles of Jesus*. Her latest book is titled: *You Can Move Your Mountains: Keep Pushing with Your Mountain—Moving Faith*.

Christine has been cited on numerous occasions for her outstanding work in the local education arena and in the D. C. and Maryland community. She was recently certified as Dean of Standard Leadership Training Schools in affiliation with the National Baptist Convention, USA, Inc., receiving her certification at the annual northeast regional conference. She served as Vice President of the District of Columbia Retired Educators Association from 2006–2008 and President-Elect 2008–2010.

Through the years, Christine has been honored as "State Vice-Principal" of the Year by The National Association of School Administrators, "Teacher of the Year" by The National Education Association, AKA Theta

Omega Omega Chapter Soror of the Year, recipient of the Regional Author's Award in 2011; Marjorie Holloman Parker Regional Award, 2007-2009; Theta Omega Omega Soror of the Year Award and the 2014 Superior Service Award and the Regional Golden Soror of the Year Award, 2020.

Currently, Christine has been inducted into the James Solomon Russell-Saint Paul's College Museum and Archives Wall of Fame. She was inducted because she made significant outstanding exemplary service and contributions to Saint Paul's College and received recognition on a regional, national, and worldwide arena. She is inducted as among the first group of inductees in the new museum and Archives. The ceremony took place during the Grand Opening, Ribbon-Cutting Service of the museum on August 10, 2019.

On November 15, 2019, on behalf of the alumni, faculty, staff, and administration of the University of the District of Columbia she was nominated and selected to receive the 2019 UDC National Alumni Society Georgia Herron Spirit award. This award recognizes alumni who exhibit superior loyalty and service to the University and the University's alumni society.